Psst

YOU HAVE A CHOICE

Psst

YOU HAVE A CHOICE

Living free:
FROM PAWN TO PLAYER

JULES PIETERS, DR. MBA.

Contents

Acknowledgments

Many thanks to everyone that has played a role in
the realization of this book:

Jet Dorhout Mees
Aimée Schellevis
Corine Scholing
Jan-Fokko Stuut
And many other special people in my life

And

Tobias, Hugo, Jasmijn and Boaz
for their unconditional inspiration

Jules

Introduction

Why keep going like this?

You say you want things to be different, but actually changing something…

You want it to be different, but you remain stuck in the patterns, the fatigue, the feeling of being out of sorts, the frustration, and perhaps even addiction.

You know it, you feel it, but still...

Is it the familiarity, the fear, the habit, or maybe your upbringing and education?

Do you live more in the past, worry about the future, and find it impossible to live in the moment?

Or is it the pressure from your surroundings and society? Is it maybe because you have to do so much… and who or what is making you do it all?

Or perhaps it's a lack of confidence, all those thoughts and judgments, or the fear of truly taking responsibility?

This book is about becoming aware, making choices, setting goals, and taking back control of your own life. In a simple, straightforward way, grounded in reality, without complicated concepts and methods. This gives you insights that are immediately applicable without the complex psychology of so-called helpers. This way, you don't move from one dependency and conditioning to another but develop true independence, self-reliance, and responsibility.

There is only one downside: there are no more excuses! After reading this book, you can never again blame anything or anyone else.

I wrote this book based on my own life experience: personal experiences and lessons such as growing up in a broken family, the early death of my father, dyslexia, school, study, sports, hobbies, and career. I have enriched these with lessons from natural religions like Vipassana, Vision Quest, and entheogenic journeys. All life lessons for which no diplomas are awarded. In this book, you will find no assumptions, concepts, theories, or stories but only the facts as I know them myself.

Of course, I realize that these facts are relative: I view them from my perspective. It is the vision I have formed, built from things I have experienced and lived through. And this vision is recognizable because I describe things that are entirely natural and that you already know deep inside. Only, over the years, you have likely often forgotten to listen to or act on them.

With the concrete tools I provide in this book, you can further develop yourself, smart and simple, direct and to the point, so that you can be your true self again in strength, authenticity, and healthy energy. From pawn to player, living in connection, freedom, and safety with care and love.

Experience it for yourself and do it, and in this way, find your home again!

So, Psst… no more excuses. Go for it. You can do it. It's your life, so do it now!

The Dimension of Time

Don't Waste Your Time

Time is a fascinating thing, and the way we handle it is a human invention. It doesn't run in sync with the rhythm and laws of nature but was created as a tool to control and manage an artificial structure. Compared to the rhythm of nature and the energy of the sun, it's a false construct. In the animal kingdom, there is a natural form of time, place, and orientation. Over the centuries, we humans have largely lost this: the inner knowing and our internal compass. We've become dependent on time zones, clocks, and watches. For economic reasons, we manipulate summer and winter each year and even add an extra day every four years.

Of course, time gives structure to our existence and initially makes mutual coordination more workable. However, the major downside of this 'artificial' time is that humanity has created a linear relationship between the past and the future. As a result, we often worry more about the past and the future, and we forget to live in the now with what truly is.

From birth, we are conditioned by upbringing and schooling. This means our lives are mainly focused on the future and, eventually, death. And this, while as newborn babies, we come into the world carefree, timeless, and rich. Just recovering from probably the biggest shock of our lives in terms of force, temperature transition, from darkness to light, and having to breathe and feed ourselves, within minutes, we lie completely satisfied on our mother's chest. And then it begins.

As parents, we have strayed so far from our natural instincts that we no longer know how to feel or act on them appropriately.

We read books, follow momfluencers, and seek help from so-called experts. We care for and raise our children based on external factors instead of on our intrinsic wisdom, and before we know it, the unnatural conditioning has begun.

To top it all off, Grandma comes along with her classic RCR belief (rest, cleanliness, and regularity) and her senile behavior, uttering things like "Coochie coo" just to get a smile from the newborn. I have never seen a creature in nature act so strangely!

We care for and raise our children according to society's norms and values. We guide – often unconsciously – more from knowledge than from inner wisdom, knowing, and nature.

We project our own personal and societal conditioning onto our offspring from the start, often from generation to generation. The result is that thinking becomes dominant and decisive. Feeling and the connection with intuition slowly fade into the background, and the pure, genuine connection gets lost.

We also often project experiences from the past onto the future. But things that have been are in the past. There's little point in worrying about or spending energy on them. Of course, it's wise to take experiences and lessons learned from the past into the present.

The future cannot be predicted however: there's no such thing as a magical crystal ball. Regardless of that, we often strive to predict, shape, control, and manage the future. We do this both in business and private life, politically, legally, religiously, economically, and even in love. We try to control it rigidly with marketing plans, budgets, marriages, and cohabitation contracts. Experience teaches us that predictions and expectations rarely come true: they stem from political, economic, and religious systems and beliefs that, upon logical and factual thinking, are based on inventions. Looking at the laws of nature, they are detached from any sense of reality.

The reality is that practice and real life have their own truths and realities. Holding on, planning, and controlling turn out to be illusions. They cost a lot of energy and usually result in frustration and an accumulation of unwanted energy, stress, illness, and, above all, a lack of freedom. I call this 'living in the horizontal dimension': living in the context of past and future. After all, nothing can be changed about the past. What has been has been.

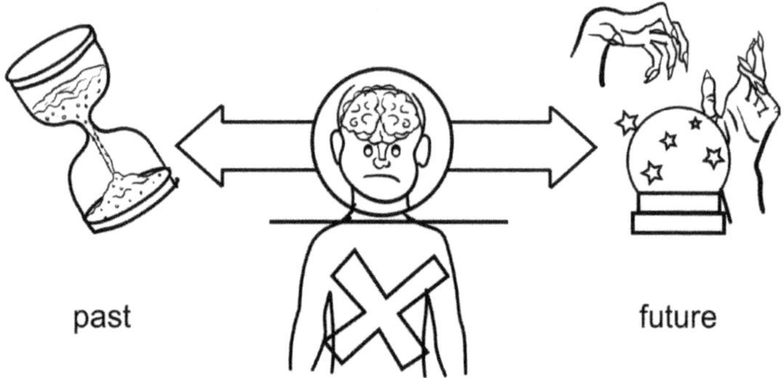

And yes, the future... I have yet to meet the fortune-teller and the prince on the white horse…

The present is the neglected child, even though it is the only absolute truth. Always here and with what is, where you are at this moment, never anywhere else!

As a counterpoint to the horizontal dimension, living in the vertical dimension is actually simple. It represents a good, healthy balance between:

Head: doing things with common sense,

Heart: connecting and caring with passion,

Gut: navigating with confidence on the inner compass: intuition.

Acting from this balanced vertical dimension shapes your life.

It is 'coming home' and 'being'. I also call it 'simply living in the dimension of being at home.'

Looking back on my life, were the decisions made from this vertical energy always right, no matter how unpredictable or initially illogical they seemed (rationally). Whether it was strolling past a theater, buying the last ticket for a show that had been sold out for months minutes before it started, or my wife's unexpected pregnancy and the birth of my eldest son, in hindsight, it all made sense.

Acting from the balanced vertical dimension often gives the feeling: I could never have imagined this, but it's perfect how it turned out. It is the magic of existence.

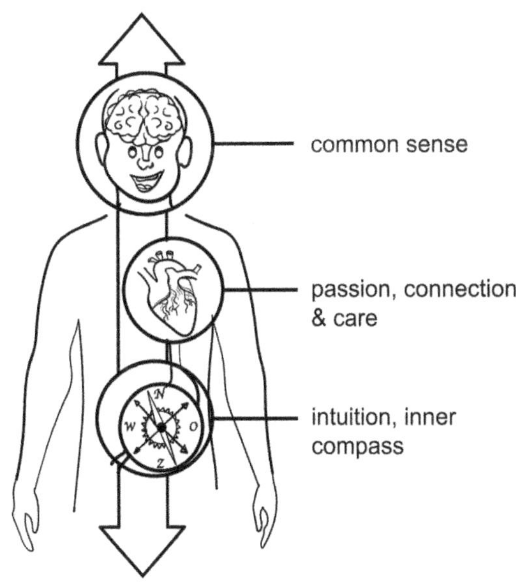

In life, we have only two certainties: we are born, and one day we will die. Don't waste the time in between. I invite you always to direct and let your energy flow. Not from hot air balloons but from the reality and truths of our existence, actual life energy with the power of 'NOW.' This requires courage and trust. It is coming home, being with what is, and *Living Life!*

Becoming Aware

Only what is, is!

I can be brief about this: only what is, is! All the rest are thoughts and stories. It might sound cliché, but there can never be anything other than what is right now.

All living beings on earth realize this. In addition, we – humans – are capable of self-awareness and observation. This is a beautiful and unique trait. We can see the whole picture and have the ability to reflect.

Due to the dominant development of our conditioning, we humans have become great storytellers, but at the same time, we have lost a large part of the essence of our existence.

Most of the stories we tell originate from fear. Fear of scarcity, fear of not being good enough, and fear of the unknown. To prevent this fear, we want to control, own/possess things, have power over something, and especially keep it.

This is also the foundation of the systems and institutions that dominate our society: politics, economy, and religion. Originally intended to serve humanity, humanity now serves them and has become subordinate to the system with its accompanying algorithms and structures.

To illustrate: no one has been able to explain the system of 'economy' to me. With my straightforward reasoning, the most essential principle of a successfully functioning economic system is that it can grow based on trust in persons or organizations.

As mentioned earlier, the future is unpredictable. When I look at the laws of nature, I don't know of any system that can only grow... Everything that grows, blooms, and lives has an end.

So, if the future is unpredictable and there is no realistic system that can only grow and be compatible with real life, how long can these beliefs and systems remain leading in our existence? How long can politics and governments keep spending more money than they receive? How many economic/banking, social, and humanitarian crises do we need before we come to our senses? When will we truly take responsibility and care for the earth and its inhabitants from a realistic perspective?

Now that the bridge to politics has been made let's move on to the straightforward reality. Democracy is a beautiful principle based on universal equality and freedom of expression. But is it really true that every person is essentially equal, both in appearance and in intelligence, knowledge, and skills? Among the billions of people on earth, no one is identical, and therefore, every individual is unique. How paradoxical is it then that no person is equal, yet it is assumed that everyone can provide the same value and have a vision on problems of various kinds, from general to complex and specialized matters. Is the democratic system essentially that the greatest orators and demagogues have the greatest attraction and thus get, have, and usually keep the power? That organizing and coordinating are based less on expertise and knowledge and more on belief and trust? And what is that trust and belief based on in reality?

Another bridge is to faith. If an almighty God exists, why have so many different books been written about it over the centuries? And if this entity exists, why has it never been seen or observed throughout the centuries? While faith can provide enormous support in belief and life, it also creates a huge dependency, especially when it comes to taking personal responsibility without shifting it onto others based on religious beliefs, rituals, and principles.

I conclude that the institutions mentioned above are not based on any logical, tangible reality. They are based on beliefs and stories and have been formed into organizations and systems with the aim of having and maintaining control and power over large groups of people.

I am still amazed that something that cannot be sustained with logical reasoning still holds, dominates society, and determines life.

Here too, the law of nature that everything is transient applies; everything comes and goes, and at the core of our existence, there is nothing to control and possess.

Simply put: The whole 'trouble' started when someone thought they could claim a piece of the earth, put a fence around it, and say: This is mine, it is 'my' property, and I have a right to it. Nowadays, we would call that plain theft!

By becoming aware of the above matters and content, you can take the first step to regain control over your own life, starting with what is, factually!

Acceptance of Reality

I Don't Want What Is,
And I Want What Isn't

The reality is that there is only what is, always is. This never changes, but in practice, I often hear and see the opposite.

We invest a lot of energy in things from the past, and we are more occupied with tomorrow than with what is now.

Whether it's about matters from the past that we keep going back to or get stuck in, or that we are primarily focused on learning for later. "If this, then that." Just three more weeks of work, and then I can go on vacation and do what I want. I am working to retire so I can start living, etc.

Of course, some things can influence the present, such as traumatic events from the past. These can still affect your autonomic nervous system in such a way that the connection in the vertical dimension no longer works naturally and healthily. This often has an unconscious and lingering impact on the present and the actions within it. Good, experienced professional help, preferably starting from the wisdom and memory of our bodies, is then necessary. Body awareness and cellular memory are the keys to restoring natural balance and trust.

Our autonomic nervous system regulates our stress system and has three strategies: fight, flight, and freeze. Such a stress reaction is often a matter of life and death and is triggered by adrenaline. In a healthy and adequate physiological response, this is quick and short-lived, and the balance is restored in a few seconds. We often see this in the form of a deep sigh, a shiver, or an intense, short-lived emotion. If the balance cannot be restored, it accumulates and disrupts the normal physiological process. This means the autonomic system is overloaded, usually as a result of unresolved (developmental) trauma.

Everyone knows the nature documentaries about the African savannah. A cheetah has its eye on a gazelle grazing nearby. The cheetah sneaks up on the unsuspecting gazelle. And then... a sprint, life-threatening danger, stress, instinctive action, focus... The gazelle is immediately full of adrenaline and runs and jumps. This time, the gazelle is too fast for the cheetah, and the latter, lacking endurance, must abandon the hunt.

An alternative strategy for the prey is to fall and play dead suddenly: 'freeze.' And since a predator does not eat dead meat, it leaves the prey alone.

Shortly after, there is a change: the prey calms down again, shivers briefly, and resumes grazing undisturbed. The nervous system is relaxed again. The cheetah continues searching for a meal or rests. Both cheetah and gazelle do not dwell on the past or fear the future.

In cases of human trauma or chronic stress, the nervous system is so overloaded that it remains in the freeze phase continuously. The connection between heart and gut can no longer be made. This creates a catch-22 situation that is difficult to escape from without expert professional help.

With healthy and natural development, without past traumas, there always is what is. There can never be anything other than what is now, here, and now in actuality! Therefore, one piece of advice: accept that because there is nothing else!

Accept what is, and you will notice that it brings peace. Acceptance doesn't mean lying back in a hammock and doing nothing. Occasionally doing nothing and loafing around is nice and can be inspiring and nourishing, but ultimately, it doesn't make your energy flow and thus doesn't enhance your happiness.

By accepting what is, you can make the next step from a free choice and thereby take control of your own life in all circumstances.

The Choice

Direct Your Energy in the Context of What Is in Life

The greatest strength of humans is our ability to perceive and experience our feelings. Many books have been written about this, often romanticized based on extreme life circumstances and experiences.

With that strength, we also have the power to change and co-create: the freedom to think, feel, react, and to choose how we handle whatever comes our way.

To me, when it comes to make choices, you always have three options:

- Continue;
- Stop;
- Do something else.

It sounds simple, and it is. We often make things too complicated, abstract, impersonal, and thus far from us removed.

I advocate 'keep it smart and simple'; it makes things understandable, applicable, and, most importantly, livable for everyone. Life is complex enough as it is.

Once you have created awareness about your situation and internal energy flow, my only advice is to accept the situation because there is nothing else than the reality of the moment.

A wise, dear friend of mine once said to me:

"Jules, to cover a mile, you have to take 1,600 steps, sometimes big, sometimes small, but you have to take each step, one after the other."

With each step, you'll experience a new situation and with that, a new experience. The invitation is to accept that and then make another choice. If it feels right and the energy flows, continue on the chosen path. If the energy is strained or doesn't feel right, you can choose to stop taking steps on that path. It may be that the path you are on is a dead end.

If the energy doesn't flow as desired, perhaps the most challenging choice is to keep taking steps, but maybe in a different direction, or perhaps with other shoes or with a different companion.

In my education and jobs, I have walked my path this way. It was often not the easiest one – whether consciously or not – and usually non-conventional. From the Dutch Mavo (now VMBO) directly to VWO, repeating years and taking four years to complete my propaedeutic phase, to ultimately, as a dyslexic, obtaining a medical degree and entering the working world.

Initially, I wanted to develop myself as a super-specialist in neurosurgery, but ultimately, I evolved through psychiatry and corporate health to where I stand now: working with the essential vitality of energy flows in people and society. The journey was intense and sometimes still feels that way because I did it as described above: continuously feeling, making choices based on those feelings, and taking responsibility outside the beaten paths or societal norms and status. And yes, that sometimes brought loneliness, and I often felt misunderstood. Walking the non-conventional path frequently evokes misunderstanding because you do not go with the masses, the norms, and prevailing mores. But, looking back, it is a price I gladly paid. This self-chosen path allows me to do the 'work' as I do it, with an important foundation of intrinsic wisdom combined with the schools and experiences of life.

Just as birth is marked by death, it is advisable to direct energy in the context of what is in life. And although it may feel somewhat paradoxical, you do need a starting point and a goal to direct and let that energy flow.

The duality is that we exist by the grace of the past and future, with the awareness and fact that the energy of this moment is the only thing that truly exists. It is the unique and essential moment of existence and thus 'Being'!

Taking Responsibility

No More Excuses

How often don't we hear, "Yeah, but I can't help it," "Yeah, but it's not my fault that it is this way," "Yeah, but it's the cause of…", "Yeah, but," "Yeah, but," "Yeah, but…"

I call this victim behavior. Of course, I'm not talking about traumatizing behavior and abuse that occurs in wars from positions of power and oppression. But even in these cases, check the books by Viktor Frankl and Edith Eger, who did not adopt a victim role despite their inhumane circumstances during World War II. The "Yeah, but" behavior I'm referring to is not wanting to take responsibility for your choices and life.

By placing decisions outside yourself or making yourself dependent on others, you avoid your responsibility. We tend to hide behind economic and legal systems, laws, and judges, and let others or the system of algorithms supposedly decide objectively or automatically.

The question is, how objective are these decisions? In reality, rules and laws appear to be open to multiple interpretations. How can it be that we have an army of lawyers in our society who use a law one day in favor of their argument and then use the same law the next day to argue against something? The same goes for a judge's ruling, which is never uniform and unequivocal: progressive judges can interpret a law differently than conservative judges, and both can come to entirely different rulings based on the same facts. If the law was above everyone and everything, there could be no difference in interpretation.

Once you become aware of an event, a feeling, or a behavior in your life, there is a choice: the choice to continue, to stop, or to do it differently. Having that choice also means there is the freedom and possibility to take control of your life and determine and lead it yourself.

You, and only you, have the privilege to make that

choice, and it can be anything you want. There is no right or wrong as long as you make the choice.

The downside of this freedom – and this is something we often forget or don't take responsibility for – is that you can't blame anyone or anything anymore. You can no longer hide behind anything! You, and only you, are responsible for your choices, regardless of the circumstances and how big or small the choice is. If every person took responsibility for themselves, society would be much simpler.

In my student street, I lived on a dead-end street: Appelstraat. Most front doors were painted in standard green and blue. Since my color blindness makes me prefer vibrant colors, I painted my front door a lovely fresh apple green. It got some looks and indirect comments, and it did indeed stand out and was a bit bright. But it was my choice, and I wasn't hurting anyone. Until a true Utrecht contractor moved in next door and soon rang my doorbell: "Neighbor, I'm getting flash blindness from your door. Do you mind if I paint it standard green?" Okay, it was my choice 😶.

So from now on, no more excuses. Choose and take responsibility for it, dare to stand up for it, and communicate!

Energy and Focus

Take Control of Your Life

In natural science, everything revolves around energy and indivisible structures, whether measurable or not. The fact remains that it exists

All chemical elements are held together and connected by physical forces. We take this for granted. At the same time, we also realize that there is much we don't know, and there is much that is intangible and unprovable.

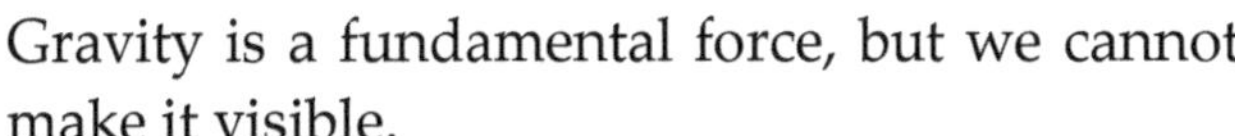

Gravity is a fundamental force, but we cannot make it visible.

We also know of the existence of large, all-consuming black holes in our solar system, but what they truly mean and entail, we do not know.

There are many phenomena and facts for which numerous leading scientists worldwide seek explanations, whether it's about the smallest Higgs particle or string theory.

Everything is energy, whether tangible and measurable or not. When energy flows, it feels natural and self-evident. When energy stagnates or comes under pressure, it feels unnatural. If we do not pay attention or take timely measures, it becomes unhealthy and possibly explosive, both literally and figuratively.

It is therefore essential to create frameworks and contexts within which energy can flow according to, and in accordance with, the laws of nature; from positive to negative, from high to low, from potential to kinetic energy, knowing that energy is never lost: the law of conservation of energy.

First, form is needed, but when energy can truly flow freely and uninhibitedly according to physical principles, it transcends form and context. That is True Living.

As self-evident as we find this in the natural sciences, we are equally critical and skeptical about our own emotions and feelings. Stimulated by our conditioning and education, we often are judgmental about them. Talking about feelings is soft, not tough, abstract, unmeasurable, etc. Navigating and steering with the energy from the heart and inner compass is experienced by many as airy-fairy, but in reality, it's the magic in our existence.

Whether it's about following your intuition or experiencing and letting energy flow, for example, in sexuality, deep down, we know it is right. It is wonderful to be with and in this energy.

It is hardly developed or stimulated, however. Immediately after birth, we are confronted with the beliefs and conditioning of our (grand)parents. In education at all levels, from preschool to university, the focus is on structure, rules, cognitive formation, and testing. Lessons and training in competence development, skills, and development in the areas of feeling, connecting, and relating are not in the curriculum, and there are no diplomas for them. Of course, they are also difficult to test ;).

The tragedy is that, after our youth, we get a sense that something is not right. The essence of qualitative existence is at a different level and has fundamentally different norms and values from what we experience. We subsequently spend the rest of our lives searching for it until we come home again: being at home, in and with ourselves.

Not every person spends the same time on this journey. There are countless songs and books written about it, but experiencing and actually living the home energy is entirely something else. A reassuring thought is that eventually, we all come home, even if it is just a second before we die.

Along the way, there are many distractions and wanderings. We numb and suppress the essence. Many hide in the system and choose to be part of the illusion, not living with the truth based on facts and the laws of nature.

Science and knowledge are wielded, and we don't live by true knowledge and knowing. Ultimately, it often comes down to financial flows, power, and political or economic interests. It is worth checking out the 'follow the money' principle.

To suppress or numb the reality and truth within ourselves, we become dependent on addictions, for example, to alcohol, (sexual) relationships, medication, sugars, social media, series, etc. This is socially accepted and elevated to the norm, but it undermines factuality and natural health. Moreover, it creates a dependency, which prevents energy from flowing freely and abundantly. On the contrary, it is toxic to your passion and intuition and thus blocks the path to true happiness, freedom, and health.

Why would you continue to suffer and drug yourself? It is relatively simple to make your own life leading again and take control of it. This allows energy to flow healthily again, provided you take responsibility with the proper focus and intention.

Sources of Energy

Do It Because You Want To, Not Because You Have To

Energy is a fascinating thing. When I talk about energy, almost everyone has some thoughts or feelings about it. At the same time, it's abstract and intangible, yet also very real.

When energy flows within us, it feels good, pleasant, lively, and connected. When it doesn't flow, we are tired, gloomy, and often suffer from mindfucks and inexplicable physical ailments.

A well-balanced energy management is essential for happiness, well-being, and good health. It's important to know your sources of energy, how to nourish them, and let the energy flow within yourself.

Healthy, balanced nutrition is widely accepted and a good foundation. Having good physical fitness also contributes to a good energy balance.

On the other hand, nicotine and alcohol are recognized

energy drainers and underminers. Both are pure poison that you put into your body, and the detoxification process to neutralize and remove them costs a lot of energy, provided you even succeed.

Excessive thinking also costs a lot of energy. 50% of our energy budget goes to our brain. So, the more pointless thoughts and worries are, the more energy is lost that you cannot use for other things.

It's important to know what you use your energy for and that you can choose to spend it differently. But it's even more interesting to look at what gives you energy and how you can realize that.

At the core, everything you do has a positive intent. Everything that touches the deeper layers within yourself gives energy. I call this being in the same frequency and vibration. Whether it's listening to Bach or hard techno, seek out energy that touches you, and you can connect with it. Seek energy that matches your frequency and align with it. Keeping the right balance between thinking, feeling, and experiencing is crucial. Whether you do that through sports, dancing, cuddling, stamp collecting, walking, or meditation, it ultimately appeals to the same thing.

Do things because you want to, not because you have to. An excellent exercise to experience this is to sit with your eyes closed in a quiet, calm environment. Then, feel. From there, think of all the things you have to do... I have to do this, I have to do that, and so on. Feel what happens to your energy level and what feeling you get from it.

Now, let go of all that 'have to' and return to a kind of neutral mindset and energy level. Now think of all the things you would like to do, things that make you happy. How does that energy feel?

You will probably notice that with 'have to,' the energy contracts and feels small, and with 'want to,' it flows and grows. See how easy it is to influence and let your energy flow? Remember the power of words. The same applies to the energy in music or other creative expressions.

This shows how you can independently influence and let your energy flow in a simple and straightforward way.

Another important significant energy source is being in and connecting with nature and its inhabitants.

If you are exhausted and full of thoughts, try taking a walk in nature. You will notice that in the first part of the walk, you are full of thoughts and judgments. You will also see and hear little of what is happening around you in nature. You might even walk right past a grazing deer without seeing it.

At some point, you will notice that those thoughts decrease, and a kind of calm arises. Your energy sinks into your body, with the main characteristic being that your breath, initially high and shallow from the chest, becomes deeper and calmer from your abdomen. When the thoughts diminish, spontaneous ideas and insights emerge from within. A problem you've been dealing with for a long time suddenly has a clear solution. An issue for which you couldn't find the right direction or the next step becomes clear. And then, at the end of the walk, a young deer might suddenly jump across your path... The energy flows, is back in balance, and everything seems to be exactly as it should be, 'now.'

Another very effective method for finding peace and letting energy flow is meditation.

To me, meditation is nothing more or less than being conscious and attentive, observing your thoughts and energy. Your primary tool here is concentration and directing your breath. Doing this consistently indeed provides inner peace.

There are also dynamic meditations where you are in motion, sometimes vigorously. Afterward, it gives the same effect of calm and energy flow.

What I often see in practice is that meditation is elevated to some kind of religion – read "belief" – and thus reduced to an instrumental thing you do once or twice a day for a few minutes. Then it's dropped, and nothing more is done with it throughout the day. Try not to get stuck in those techniques and beliefs. Instead, do things consciously and attentively throughout the day, not just during a set period.

Meditation should not be seen as something 'elevated' or elevated to religion because that defeats its purpose. A nice walk in nature, a good workout, an evening of dancing, or a pleasant lovemaking session have the same effect ;)

In summary, you can say that anything that uses your senses and pushes thinking to the background ensures that energy flows. When you use your senses, you are not able to think or form thoughts. So go and experiment creatively with feeling, tasting, hearing, seeing, and smelling in any form that suits you. Connect with the elements of nature like air, water, earth, and fire. This can be done at home on the couch or through an activity.

Do everything with attention and awareness, and you will notice that the energy in your system flows freely and healthily.

And most importantly: Don't think, just do!

The Power of Breath and Intrinsic Knowledge

The Tool to Reconnect with Yourself

Our breath is one of the most powerful 'tools' we have at our disposal. The beauty of it is that it's always available to you; you can use it anytime and anywhere, and it's completely free.

The first thing we do as humans when we come out of our mother's womb is take a deep breath. This brings everything to earthly life. And even the last thing we do before we die is breathe.

Remarkably, our initial and final breaths come deeply from our belly. These are not hindered by stories and thoughts, which make breathing shallow and bring it upwards. And at the end of life, the last breath is one of complete surrender.

How is it that something so essential to our life and also to the quality of life has been forgotten? Is it because we often tend not to pay attention to what we take for granted? Whether it's taking good care of yourself, your health, or your relationship and love. Is it because of the conditioning and dominance of the development of the intellect, the knowledge, and less attention to skill and competency development?

And this while breathing is so essential and inextricably linked to our life, even being the great motor of our energy management, well-being, and health.

From my perspective, it is because, in our Western culture, the focus is so much on the cognitive that breathing becomes subordinate. In Eastern philosophies, breath/life energy gets more attention from childhood through exercises and habits like qi-gong, yoga, meditation, tantra, etc. Doing things with attention is also more connected and identified with life there. It simply belongs to life and is integrated into daily maintenance like eating, drinking, and self-care. It is also a sexual energy flow and life energy. The paradox is that in those countries, materialism and thinking are slowly taking the lead, with all the negative consequences. The earth and its natural resources are being plundered and burdened even more.

The striking aspect here is that historically, the West has often tried to dominate the East, claiming with a certain arrogance to have the ultimate wisdom. As I see it, power and economic gain are the most significant drivers and the dominant energy here. It is more about quantity and less about the quality of life. Money and possessions can indeed bring happiness, but you and I also know deep down that true happiness is really about other energies and things, like connection, safety, friendship, and love.

In the East, you see more and more of a longing for materialism and individualism. Through various temptations and marketing of all material things, an external need is created, and desires are increased. The new belief is focused on the pursuit of those things, especially future-oriented, supposedly making you happy. The tragedy here is that there is no realization of what it truly costs. Namely, that matter and possessions at their core do not truly make you happy but make you dependent, with the opposite result. The society of connectedness and caring for each other crumbles, and the gap between rich and poor only gets bigger. The migration to big cities – supposedly because wealth is to be found there – remains the goal, with all the consequences that entails. Often, it results in a life of abuse, poverty, and living in slums. However, in practice, quantitative wealth does not outweigh qualitative wealth. The tragedy is that the way back is difficult to walk. It remains remarkable to see that the intrinsic wisdom of being connected to another dimension of life and energy remains present, giving people support and hope.

Here, connected breathing is an essential foundation.

It is, for example, beautiful to see how, on an island like Bali, the original culture remains intact in its uniqueness and offerings, while Westerners flood the island on scooters with an 'external energy' of showing off, 'living the life.'

In Western society, qualitative energies are becoming important again. Yoga schools have sprung up like mushrooms, courses in mindfulness, meditation, and tantra can be found in every city, and the acceptance and role of mind-expanding substances are becoming more and more accepted. The realization of the power and essential nature of good breathing is an important common thread.

Unfortunately, I also see it being done and experienced instrumentally. This places it outside of oneself instead of integrating it into your original natural system and your daily energy and breathing.

In Eastern philosophy and society, it is more accepted to consult and listen to wisdom and life experience. It is common to have a teacher or shaman with a natural standing and acceptance. While it is an entirely natural fact that one person has more wisdom and life experience than another, we find that difficult to accept in the West. The conditioned misconception here is that it is not about being better or worse, not about being dumber or smarter, but about competencies and skills with which a person is born and has developed and mastered in life. Again, it is about life quality and skill, not quantity and possession.

Ultimately, there will be a balance with less distinction but more individuality and authenticity. Historically, everything comes and goes in waves. The symbol of yin and yang is a beautiful example of this, with the preservation of identity.

I want to invite you to pay attention to your breathing and feel what happens within your system. You will experience that the main effect is that you will be more and more connected in the vertical time dimension energy and thus with an inner balance and calmness.

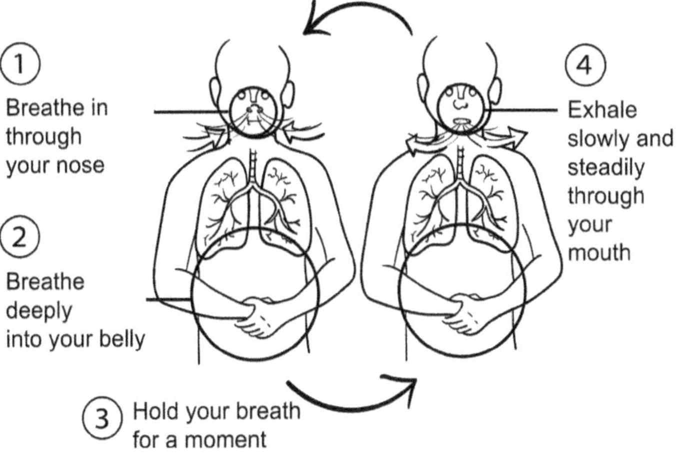

Practice and play with your breathing in intensity, frequency, and depth. Consciously and calmly, breathe through your nose with your hands on your belly. Hold it there for a moment, and then exhale calmly but steadily through your mouth. As a framework, you can create a structure for yourself of inhaling for 4-7 counts, resting for 2-4 counts, exhaling for 4-7 counts, resting for 2-4 counts, and so on. The important thing is to find a natural rhythm for yourself and not follow an external scheme because it is supposed to be that way! A few minutes a day is enough to get familiar with it. And once you have that, you own, once and for all, in any situation or environment, the most powerful tool to reconnect with yourself and experience calmness. This gives you the choice to stay close to yourself and act with the appropriate next step and direction for you.

Fear and Undermining Thoughts

Look at What Is
Instead of What Isn't

Fear is one of the most undermining energies for a high-quality life. It usually involves the fear of lacking, the fear of not being enough, and the fear of death.

These thoughts of fear are illogical and unnatural.

Fear and not being enough have apparently been learned and have become conditioning, even the norm. The source lies in your upbringing and education. Unconsciously and unintentionally, but still a direct consequence. It starts at birth with your parents, after which it is quickly taken up in daycare centers and schools. At birth, there is no fear of life. You are perfectly fine as you are, here and now. In fact, you are a great source of inspiration and love for your surroundings. But your upbringing pulls you more and more out of that energy of your natural state or throws you out of the ocean of love. You must adhere to the prevailing sleep and eating rhythms. You must do this and that and may no longer do such and so. You have to sleep and eat a certain number of times, sit still, and finish your plate. If you draw a blue tree and a black sun, corrective remarks are made, or an appointment is made with a psychologist because something must be wrong with you, as a tree is really green and the sun is yellow. You are conditioned to conform to the masses and prevailing norms and values. This causes you to lose more and more of your inner connection, creativity, and originality. Everything is focused on knowledge and performance and, above all, not stepping out of line. The development of your passion and inspiration from intrinsic creativity and wisdom fades into the background and is hardly, if ever, called upon.

And all this under the pretext: 'We know what is good for you.' Parents, governments, scientists, and institutions all do this.

As a result, we often spend a lifetime realizing that we are perfect as we are and were, always on the way, sometimes successfully, and sometimes making mistakes, but nothing is more human than that. What has been made personal from early childhood is, in reality, never personally attributable to the actual person.

When we look at fear, there is never a real reason to be very afraid of anything. In fact, there may only be one real fear in our lives, which is the fear of dying prematurely. And even then, even before the moment of death approaches, all fear is gone even though death is our only certainty and anchor in our existence!

The natural balance and proportion are out of balance. Everyone can have that awareness, but because it has often become so faded, we ignore the core of the problem and continue on the same path. Everyone knows it: it's so distant from me, and I don't have to deal with it personally, that an attitude of 'whatever' arises. Think of wars, air and sea pollution, poverty, attacks, the virus pandemic, and the unequal distribution of wealth and resources. Does one person have more right to live than another? When asked, we all say: "of course not; look at the basic human rights." But when it really hits home, we don't know how fast we need to start acting, especially out of self-interest.

The reality is that the world is not fair and equal. We all try hard to maintain that: butter on our heads and blinders on. And the primary motivation behind that is fear.

The reality is that most shortages are created by ourselves. If we look at the big picture, the earth is rich in food and resources. There is enough space to live and enough resources to provide our food supply. But we want more and more, and at its core, we abuse our natural resources and stocks. A painful consequence of this is that there is a lot of overproduction, and much of our natural energy sources are wasted through overconsumption. The result is that much of the cultivated food is not consumed and just goes to waste. One-third of all produced food is wasted! The same applies to many goods, such as clothing – often made in China – which end up unused in landfills, partly due to impersonal online shopping and the convenience of returns.

What a waste of energy and resources, and what an injustice to humanity and countries where poverty and a lack of basic necessities such as clean drinking water and healthy hygiene still prevail.

The fact that the rich are getting richer economically, wanting to possess more and maintain power, ensures that the poor become poorer and more dependent and remain that way. This, consciously or unconsciously, maintains a fertile ground for fear.

What we can really suffer from is the often unconscious fear of unprocessed emotions and old pains built up in our system. Eckhart Tolle beautifully described these as so-called pain bodies. These are still lingering energies in our system that can be 'triggered' by something that happens. Unconsciously, we have suppressed them, but it is still possible to be affected by them.

Have you ever wondered why something doesn't affect you at all, and you can let it go by without any problem, while at another moment, something deeply affects and hurts you? In the latter case, there is a good chance that an old, unprocessed energy is being touched.

If I say: gosh, you have an ugly nose, there is a good chance you think: keep that comment to yourself, or who do you think you are to say that? You don't let it harm your energy. But if it makes you angry or sad, there is a good chance that something old is being touched. That there was an impact on your appearance in the past that hasn't been processed, and a negative, draining energy is still attached to it.

Perhaps you've heard that children are your most excellent teachers? It's precisely for this reason. Children, no matter how young, are still so uninhibited and can evoke the most intense emotions in you. That cannot possibly come from their expressions and actions, let alone be personally directed at you. So, the fact that you are touched is, by definition, not from the present but from something old. Because the connection with children is based on unconditional love, you cannot ignore it, and they are your most fantastic mirror.

If something touches you that you can't really place or want to place outside yourself, it is essentially an invitation to accept the touch and deal with it consciously this time. By doing so, you transform this energy and regain your freedom.

The unconscious fear of something that touched you comes from old pain. It makes you inherently unfree and stagnates the energy within you, whether consciously or unconsciously.

The key and solution to something that touches you profoundly is to feel it without judgment and examine it with attention. Through self-examination and conscious breathing, the energy can change and flow freely and healthily again. It is like a profound and essential cleansing and clearing!

In conclusion, fear is usually a story. At its core, it is something you are afraid of. Something that might happen in the future, even though it rarely, if ever, happens for real. Look back at your life. How often have you been afraid of something that actually happened? And how frequently have you dreaded something and said afterward: "Well, I really didn't need to feel scared or uncertain about that"?

It is usually the story and thoughts beforehand, stemming from something in the past, that are projected into the future, completely ignoring the actuality and reality. As said, in the actuality of the moment, there is usually nothing to be afraid of!

Fear is a very undermining and freedom-robbing energy based on assumptions. The consequences are immense and hinder a qualitatively worthy life.

And suppose the fear becomes so great that you think you can no longer handle it. In that case, you see something remarkable happen: either you fall entirely into numbness or psychosis, or more likely, all fears disappear, and there is a complete surrender to what is: the truth and nothing but the truth. The Now. In this surrender, the fear is no longer present in your system.

By releasing old pain and fear through proper breathing and awareness and letting go of the thoughts of not being good enough, you take an essential step towards a free and qualitatively richer life!

Practically speaking, look in connection with reality, at what is, instead of what isn't.

Of course, I haven't been spared from fears that have (had) an impact on my perception and physical system and thus on my quality of life. A good example of this is the feeling of acrophobia. Something I have felt naturally from a young age, even though I wasn't born with it. My children don't suffer from it, and that became all the more clear during a vacation in France and visiting a climbing forest. You know it: various courses and obstacles at different heights in a beautiful natural environment between the trees. My children took one obstacle after another like 'monkeys' and nonchalantly called: "Dad, come, join us!"

It was confronting because nothing is more beautiful than making memories with your loved ones. The reality, however, was that I was nailed to the ground, holding my breath at the nonchalance with which the children went through the obstacles. I kept breathing consciously to avoid projecting my fear onto them. I didn't want to spoil their fun and speed by attempting to try it myself as a trembling snail.

That I had the perception and awareness but couldn't bear the cramp of fear in my system, knowing it was a thought/story, was hugely confronting.

It led me to decide to invite a very sporty yogi friend to visit a local climbing forest on a quiet weekday to explore my fear. To cut it short, the first course at 40 cm height took about an hour. However, with the built-up confidence, feeling well, and breathing, I could transform my thoughts into the experience of trust. After that, no height or obstacle was too difficult. I even enjoyed it so much that my athletic friend, now somewhat less confident, cautiously suggested halfway through the course: "Jules, maybe it's time to go home and use the ladder to get down?" ;)

The same feeling still regularly returns, such as at the beginning of the paragliding season and the first altitudes above the earth again. However, with the accumulated experience and awareness, these thoughts that can undermine my sense of security are increasingly easier to transform into being with what is in reality and enjoying and playing with it.

Duality and
Who Observes What

As Humans, We Can Perceive
and Observe Ourselves

Have you ever realized that you can observe your own thoughts? That you can see yourself doing something, or hear yourself saying something? That you can perceive and experience yourself as if you are outside of yourself? That you realize you are dreaming? That you realize you are sad, in pain, happy, etc.? And all of this from a position as an observer of yourself?

Have you ever realized that if you observe something, you essentially cannot be that something yourself? The object, the person, is unique, but to be able to observe, it must 'be' outside itself to observe and perceive.

It is remarkable that we, as humans, are manifest in who we are, but that apparently, something outside of us exists that observes both our body and our thoughts. Some people refer to it as an 'out-of-body experience.'

For me, it is not an experience but something that is continuously present.

There is a duality between what is and what observes. There is always something that registers and considers, but what 'is' that then?

One step further, everyone knows the 'déjà vu' feeling. A situation or environment in which you find yourself and suddenly realize: I've been here before, or I've seen or experienced this before, even though you've never been in that situation or environment before. Yet, you have seen it before, perhaps in a vivid dream. At that moment, it was not real, but sometimes, days or years later, it turns out to be factual and real.

Déjà vu is an example of something that is real and works but for which there is (yet) no suitable explanation. I find it fascinating. Yes, I am familiar with some theories from mystics who claim to have an explanation for this, but again, that is on the level of beliefs and assumptions.

Let's look at this perception and experience as if watched through the lens of a cinema movie. A projector projects the image with light onto a screen. We can become completely absorbed in the movie, but an observer from the outside does not see the movie, but the light, the film, the projector, and the screen on which the image becomes visible.

In our lives, who or what is the light? Are we as humans 'the film,' and is this combination what we experience and can perceive?

Everything is inextricably connected, and one cannot exist without the other. The dot made with a pencil exists by the grace of the paper on which it is placed. And there are many other examples: light-dark, sweet-sour, joy-sorrow, woman-man, sound-silence, yin-yang, sending-receiving, and so on. They are all sides of the same coin, ultimately forming a unity, the all-one! One cannot exist without the other; they are inextricably linked.

When we realize this and also experience, see, and accept the other side of the coin, it brings peace and wholeness to everything that is in our lives. Staying stuck or only realizing and acknowledging one side of the coin brings unrest, dependency, and struggle because it does not align with reality. Peace comes when we can experience the merging and acceptance in duality, both in form and in energy, or even transcending the form. That is why intimacy and sexuality play such a prominent role in our lives, and at the same time, can feel so unfree and hidden because we have not learned to deal with them naturally.

When we do not want to see or acknowledge that duality, we tend to drug ourselves with addictions on various fronts. Ultimately, however, that only fosters emptiness and increases the distance between the two sides of the duality.

When the duality converges and blends, it can feel like coming home within ourselves, being whole in acceptance and connection with our environment.

The conclusion is that there is a duality in our human existence. It is a fact that there is an 'object' human and that there is an abstract observer who registers: an unknown entity/energy outside of ourselves.

The fact that we as humans can perceive and observe ourselves distinguishes us - at least as far as I know - from all other life on our beautiful planet Earth. And the beauty is that from that observation and awareness, there is always the possibility to make a choice.

Perhaps the greatest mystery of our humanity in the 21st century is that there is more between heaven and earth, based on reality and not on belief. Or does everything eventually disappear into the all-consuming black holes of our universe, and is everything 'already whole'?

Competence, Passion, and Bliss

Isn't It Time to Choose What Is Important to You?

Following your heart and traveling as a hero might seem like abstract words. However, the work and ideas of the scholar Joseph Campbell have truly explored and described the human experience in these terms.

It is challenging to write and say things that are not measurable and perhaps not reproducible. Yet, they can feel factual and true because they are.

Are emotions and feelings like tears, falling in love, reproductive feelings, heart-stopping fright, roaring laughter, and so on, objectively and physiologically explainable? Just as pain, both mental and physical, exists in so many different forms, intensities, and experiences. We all know it, but is it really objectively definable and explainable?

The same applies to concepts like competence and passion. Feeling and experiencing where your talent lies, what makes you happy, perhaps without any formal education or training, is a natural given and skill.

However, within the regular school system, there is hardly any time or space offered to explore this, let alone develop it. This makes it difficult for young people to feel and choose a field where their talents can shine and grow. On the other hand, you are expected to profile yourself in a particular field.

It is so easily said that you should do what you are good at. Yet, you must choose certain subjects at school when you are just 14 or 15 years old. The guiding factor is grades, which hardly say anything about someone's actual competencies and talents. How can you learn or explore what truly makes you happy and what you are good at to possibly pursue it professionally later, if the entire education system is not designed to discover, develop, and stimulate that?

I never understood why, in a field like medicine, primarily selection criteria are cognitive skills when a competent doctor absolutely needs social skills, with the potential to develop a gut feeling of 'something is or isn't right.'

And if we find our school system so fitting and aligned with what our society needs, how can it be that about 70% of the population works in a field unrelated to their education?

We are trained to focus on things outside ourselves and unlearn to follow our heart and passion. We have even become afraid to do so and lack confidence. But by following our inner impulses and doing things where the energy flows, we come into our own and become more qualitatively meaningful to our environment and society. By acting from inner strength, we become autonomous and much less dependent on environmental factors, and conditions like burnout will become a rarity.

So, I would like to ask you the following questions:

- Are you happy with the work you do and the environment in which you do it?
- Are you aware of your talents, what makes you happy, and what is your passion?
- Is the role shaped by your choices and education still the right fit for you?

If you answered yes to these three questions, then you are likely a happy and healthy person who enjoys life.

If you answered no to one or more questions, then I ask you to consider why you do the things you spend most of your time on, even though they don't feel right. Do you do things because others expect them of you, because you have been conditioned to, or is it the fear of...?

Isn't it time to choose what is truly important and nourishing for you?

Don't let yourself be held back any longer, and start doing things where your energy again flows naturally. And when the energy can flow in the right direction without fear, you'll experience satisfaction and happiness.

I wish you all the courage and confidence in this journey!

Love... and Life

Love is the Most Special
Free Energy in Our Lives

Love is inextricably linked to the quality of life and our humanity.

When I talk about love, everyone immediately knows what I mean; there is an instant recognition in feeling and imagery. Despite this universality, chances are we all have very diverse experiences, feelings, and images associated with it and give it different meanings. This also makes love so complex. Here too, the essence and factuality are simple, and it is the stories and fears from 'past to future' that cause the complexity.

So, what is the meaning of love if everyone knows it and has a clear feeling about it?

I distinguish between two interpretations of love. Well, two, in essence and purity, there is only one real form, which I call true pure love. This energy is unconditional, cannot be influenced or possessed, and is universal and undeniable.

The birth of my children made me truly realize, experience, and recognize this love again. It brings a wealth of experiences that can be experienced in no other way. Only by going through it can you truly experience its essence. With children and the experiences involved, the most important thing is experiencing unconditional love and the confrontation with a flawless mirror for my own regular incapacity with feelings and thoughts. It is also a privilege to witness the richness of primal strength, instincts, and inner wisdom.

You don't 'take' children; they happen. From a hopefully loving act and the possible subsequent fusion, an egg cell meets a sperm cell. From that fusion of cells, a completely new human being with all its features develops in nine months. Then the time comes when that new wonder of life wants to go out of the womb and lead its own life after a process of primal force and emotions, the birth.

From that moment on, women and men become parents and are connected in that capacity for life. This creates a parent-child relationship that never disappears. In other words, a love and bond arise that is unconditional and cannot be severed. No matter what happens in the relationship, how good or bad, this bond will exist for a lifetime.

In everything, I say: take care of yourself first because otherwise, you have nothing to give. An empty battery cannot provide power. However, in a parent-child relationship, the parent will always take care of a (dependent) child first. Even if the flight attendant can explain the safety procedures before takeoff in a plane and say you must put on your oxygen mask first and then that of your child, in an emergency, no matter how irrational it is, your primary instinct is to care for your child first.

I often use the image: if someone crosses the street while a car is coming, I will shout and try to prevent it. But if a young child does it, I will do everything possible to pluck the child from the street, even at all costs to myself, unconditionally!

Then there is what I call 'cow-trade love': the love that, in today's society, has been elevated to the norm, whether it is love within relationships or love for a faith or god.

Love for a god can only be professed according to the teachings of that institution, often worded in a complex book and story. Unfortunately, these usually beautiful ancient scriptures can be interpreted in multiple ways, and there is no unequivocal truth and factuality. That was clear in the past and still is, thinking of all the crusades and (current) wars fought because of faith.

As for common love relationships, the facts also seem clear. From romance, infatuation, and perhaps lust, the relationship often begins. When Cupid hits the mark, we are on a cloud that seems untouchable. But over time, no matter how wonderful and memorable this energy is, the cloud turns out to be not so solid and can also bring thunder and lightning.

Friction, misunderstanding, and inaccessibility arise, and most love relationships end. If romance leads to marriage with the promise of eternal fidelity, nowadays, about 40-50% end in divorce. I honestly wonder why those who remain married stay together, maybe except for social, economic, legal, or other reasons, usually children. And then I'm not even talking about the percentage of people who have intimate relationships with others outside their 'unique' love connection, usually secretly and not transparently.

How many marriages do you know that, after decades, are still loving, nurturing, inspiring, free, energetic, and sparkling, where the partners bring out the best in each other in safety and security?

The origin of cow-trade love relationships lies in the fact that you seek or compensate for your own deficiencies in the other. So, something of yourself that you don't have or dare to live, you find in the other person, allowing you to experience it. It gives a feeling of wholeness, but it is one with a dependence on one another. That is why people in love often say they feel so good and complement each other, they understand each other so well, they are really meant for each other, and they show and share that (grandly) with the world.

What they do not realize is that they are undermining the free, autonomous love relationship. Because if you depend on something or someone, there will inevitably come a time when you must say goodbye to it again.

As mentioned earlier, the law of nature is that everything comes and goes, and everything is transient. This is also true in relationships, whether by choice or by parting through death; the physical relationship in earthly existence ends at some point.

Most people are unaware of this, and a claim can arise on the partner – often in the area of intimacy/sexuality, she/he is mine – or through a usually unconscious fear of being alone again. Old energies, such as not being good enough, can then be triggered. This creates an increasing degree of unfreedom and loss of authenticity, which causes friction or stagnation in energy. This then evokes anger, frustration, unhappiness, etc. The consequences and impact on relationships can be seen around us daily, usually in the form of indifference, struggle, and impotence.

Relationships evolve, and norms and values change

as well. Young people act very differently from their parents and grandparents. This does not change the fact that becoming aware of your feelings and thoughts is essential for entering a healthy love relationship. A relationship where primary care and unconditional love for yourself are the foundation. From that basis, freedom and autonomy can be shared and extended to the other without being dependent on it for your own happiness and love. First, healthy unconditional love for yourself, then with someone else!

Another undermining factor for the conventional concept of marriage is that humans evolve. Men and women are increasingly reaching an equal level, both socially and within a relationship and family. Increasing awareness and healthy emancipation of both men and women doesn't work well with the marriage system and its origin, causing friction and tension.

Also, as humans, we are living longer, meaning we are, in principle, connected to a single person for a longer time. The fact is that humans evolve, but the system remains rigid and is still promoted by faith and government. Practical and legal adaptations lag behind development and need, undermining flowing loving energy, a catch-22.

I genuinely wonder why institutionalizing love still takes such a prominent place in our society.

My underlying thought is that perhaps the establishment and religious leaders have an interest in maintaining systems of conditioned habits and customs.

With these unnatural systems and their 'invented' norms and values, a system is created to maintain control and power over society and its subjects. Illustratively, you can usually get married for free in five minutes on a Monday morning, but to divorce, you need a lawyer. However, to divorce, the request must be submitted to a judge for approval.

Love for and the urge to live are so elemental and essential that no matter how dire the situation, people always keep going. In cases of suicide, this usually happens out of psychological distress, stagnant life energy, not being able to feel and see: depression. This literally suppresses feelings and energy and, thus, makes them no longer connected to life.

How remarkable is it then that suicide rarely, if ever, occurs among people living in terribly inhumane conditions, such as homeless people, people in war situations, prison camps, poverty, and those lacking food and drink? Apparently, even in those circumstances, where objectively there is little to no quality of life, people still experience a source and energy that is so strongly connected to life that they do not break the line through self-destruction.

Love is grand and essential in its truth for and with yourself, independent of anyone or anything. As said, love cannot be possessed or owned. Love is the most extraordinary free energy in our lives. It is the most critical source of quality of life in any form. We are born with it, and we die with it.

Connecting and Relating

Pure Communication Can Only Happen from Authenticity

Love and care for ourselves are the most essential things for a high-quality life. When this is in order, we can also be meaningful to others. Only after taking care of our own energy and health can we start sharing and reaching out without shortchanging ourselves.

Ayn Rand wrote the novel "The Fountainhead" early in the last century, in which he beautifully and narratively described the importance of authenticity: standing up for yourself with the dynamic and essential difference between altruism and healthy egoism.

As I interpret it, altruism is doing good according to prevailing norms and values. This places the focus outside ourselves, often accompanied by manipulation and power to maintain this external focus. It is mainly directed at the exterior, providing service for the greater good. What is usually forgotten is that at the top of that greater good, only a few make the decisions and determine how much room you have to move.

Healthy egoism is about taking good care of yourself first in terms of health and well-being. When this is balanced, and you are able to be authentic and independent, you can take up space from which you can share. This allows you to be truly meaningful to people, society, and the world. This has nothing to do with so-called antisocial behavior, as religions and governments would often have us believe. They prefer 'docile' to autonomous, free-thinking, and acting individuals.

I want to translate this into relating and communicating from person to person in all forms. Communication takes place according to the principle of sending and receiving. When one speaks, the other listens, and vice versa. But as soon as we start interpreting and thinking for someone else, there is noise. The respect and purity of sharing with the other are lost. And if people start transmitting simultaneously without alignment, there is no reception, creating chaotic energy in between.

Before pure communication can take place, it is necessary to have a good inner connection, as described in the energy of the vertical dimension.

This means you need to know yourself thoroughly, know your strengths and weaknesses, and be aware of them. When communicating from within this dimension, you can share with authenticity and purity.

The receiver must also stand autonomously and independently to receive purely and objectively.

What does not work, and unfortunately often happens, is sharing and receiving from impurity, thinking for the other, or dependency, whether consciously or unconsciously.

Pure communication and consultation on an issue or topic can only happen from authenticity and respect. This way, you can relate and communicate openly and honestly with each other.

If we drop things unasked onto someone's plate without any alignment, we disrespect that person.

If we think for the other person and start communicating from there, it becomes storytelling and not communicating from facts and authenticity. Also, if we share something but actually expect or want something in return, it creates impurity and murkiness.

Perhaps most importantly, when we speak and share from a personal emotional reaction, it is wiser to take responsibility for that emotion first and only communicate once you have removed its charge.

All these things make pure and connected communication almost impossible. All the impurities often lead to more confusion and misunderstanding.

A beautiful way of sharing is to place a topic in a virtual bowl between you and your conversation partner.

You share a genuine opinion or vision by putting it in the bowl. The other has the freedom and choice to look at what is in the bowl without it being dropped unasked onto their plate. If this happens in mutual energy and agreement, you can discuss what is in 'the bowl' without making it personal. This way, pure and transparent consultation and communication can take place.

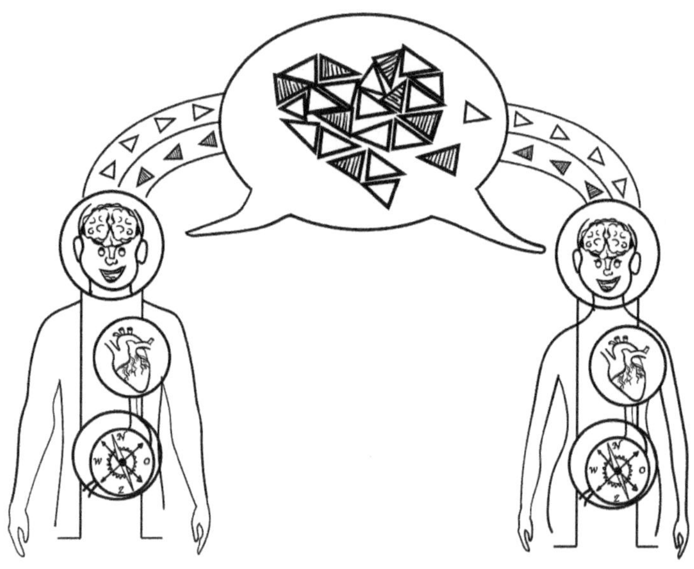

What also muddies and confuses relations and communicating is placing responsibilities outside yourself, or 'you-butting': blaming the other or your environment. "You always do this; you are the cause of that. It's definitely not my fault. If only you would... you, you you." This way, you do not take responsibility for your thoughts, feelings, choices, and actions and project your personal incapacity, sensitivity, and shortcomings onto the other.

This has two significant consequences: you place something outside yourself over which you have no influence, and you drop something unasked onto someone else's plate without checking if it is welcome.

How different it is if you take responsibility and care for yourself and share from your personal energy.

This has two consequences: you keep things with yourself and thus also take responsibility, and you place something neutrally on someone else's plate, giving them the choice to act on it or not. Only this way, pure, clear, and sincere communication is possible. No matter how complex or loaded the subject is, with these 'rules,' you don't get tangled in a web of struggle and incapacity.

So, unconditional care for your own house and garden comes first, where you decide who has access and who may stay. The same applies, of course, to the other person's house and garden, where you respect the boundaries.

For this, there must be awareness from a meaningful and loving upbringing to know what your house and garden mean and what their contents and boundaries are.

In the 21st century, this has become complex, given the role, influence, and dominance of social media. Connections and relationships seem to have been reduced to digital and somewhat anonymous contacts. Moreover, influencers create images that have little to do with reality and natural laws. It has become a hype to gain as many followers as possible or to be part of them to belong digitally. Thus, a surrogate 'catch-22' is created: more followers mean more income, and to get more followers, more unnatural videos are made, and more people watch those videos to belong, etc. An utterly illusory world without a real-world connection has emerged, all from your screen at home, preferably in a horizontal position ;)

I had the privilege of making an Atlantic crossing on a sailing ship with 37 young people between 14 and 17 years old, aka teenagers! Part of that project was that these young people did not have access to their mobile phones for most of the time on the sailing ship. It is fantastic to see what fun, originality, innovative playfulness, and responsibility arose in the connections and interactions. I experienced and saw the sparkle and joy in these young people. It is a beautiful and rich illustration of the natural connection in what is.

As already mentioned, governments and institutions are handling more and more important matters. This makes them impersonal and abstract, and the actual seeing, feeling, and speaking to each other disappears. By anonymizing and digitizing the human factor in systems, the natural principle of truly seeing, knowing, connecting, and caring for each other disappears.

A beautiful illustrative example is the so-called Dutch bread funds. These are transparent systems where entrepreneurs/self-employed people take care of each other in case one of them is temporarily incapable of working. It is based on personal connection and trust. The practical success and enormous growth in recent years show that this system works well.

Politics is starting to interfere here as well, and there are calls to mandate self-employed people to take out insurance, supposedly for the protection and care of the group. This removes all responsibility and creates an anonymous institution where control and lack of trust play a dominant role.

The same example applies to health insurance. We have made health and the care for it one of our most significant qualitative rights. We have established a legal obligation to have health insurance and a tax system that finances it. Within this system, you have become a number instead of a person as a human being. Accessing the healthcare system, especially its financing, has become anonymous.

Meanwhile, we find it self-evident that medical help is provided in case of illness or deficiency. However, addressing someone about their lifestyle, which is often an underlying cause, is considered an invasion of privacy and unethical. Illustrative here are diseases like Type II diabetes (old age diabetes) and cardiovascular diseases. Being overweight and having an unhealthy lifestyle are directly related to the development of ailments. In fact, when lifestyle and weight become normal again, chronic medical treatment is usually no longer necessary! Unfortunately, it has now become self-evident that we treat symptoms without addressing the actual cause.

Then, there is the role of so-called coaches and psychologists in our society. These are actually a consequence of our current upbringing and the schooling system. During our upbringing and education, we essentially forget to think and feel for ourselves. It is also not developed and taught. We are trained to acquire and reproduce knowledge, not to build and refine skills. When it comes to personal development and emotional issues, we are hardly given any skills or tools.

Since we ultimately need balance, sooner or later, there will be a reason or necessity to do something about it. However, because during our regular development process, aspects of our potential often remain untouched, people frequently seek help and knowledge from these supposedly socially recognized 'experts.'

What was once learned, carried, and resolved within a community is now institutionalized under the guise of discretion and privacy. The study of psychology is booming today, and seeking help from psychologists and coaches, with the accompanying waiting lists, is illustrative. Unfortunately, I conclude that often, no real help, skills, or insights are provided, let alone tools, to actually change independently and qualitatively. Also, within mental health care, I see more symptom treatment than addressing the actual cause.

This makes sense since the same education and theories shape that group of psychologists themselves. There is little evidence of individuality, life experience, and personal skill development within these studies. Guidance is provided from learned theories, conceptually, and hardly any from personal strength. The intrinsic presence of power and energy in our own body of wisdom and knowledge and its functioning are not taught and studied at universities. This way of help and guidance, and the so-called therapies linked to it, creates and maintains unfreedom and dependency. This is contrary to shaping life based on the insights and facts as I have described.

I won't even discuss the hype of the role of coaches and their guidance. Most of it is based on and focused on the exterior, external empowerment, sociological tricks, and marketing. It is actually a form of deception because sharing and teaching a trick does not last long, is superficial, and therefore has a short-term effect. The deeper, essential layers and skills remain untouched. Disillusionment and dissatisfaction are the result. Soon, we look for the next training, pep talk seminar, coach, or self-help dummy book. Fundamental transformation and learning intrinsic skills and competencies to gain true control over your life are not addressed.

Of course, there are exceptions; people who have been shaped by life have faced their challenges independently from confirmations and prevailing mores: people who can support, guide, and provide insights from their experience and wisdom. With them, authenticity, involvement, and independence are tangible, without personal interest or existential claim. These people are independent and do not need to hide behind theories, professional groups, or anything else. Loving, involved, authentic, with common sense and a great feeling in 'being' and acting.

Setting Goals and Charting a Course

Without a Goal, Energy Cannot Flow

To allow energy to flow in love and connection, you need frameworks and a direction within which the energy can flow. And to experience direction, you need to set a goal. This may feel contradictory because setting a goal is always future-oriented. You can never know in advance if you will actually achieve or realize that goal.

As already mentioned, there really is only 'this' moment in your life. This is understandable and can be felt. You need to realize that this moment can only exist in the context of the past, what has been, and a future that is yet to come.

Focusing our lives only on the one certainty of the future, death, is a waste. That does not mean that the present does not exist due to this force field of past and future, allowing us to live in it. Comparable to an electron that is always in its place but always in motion, full of energy in a force field between a potential difference of plus and minus.

Without setting a goal, energy cannot flow.

Clear frameworks are needed to allow energy to flow freely and healthily. By this, I mean taking up space with authentic self-care. If the environment does the same, you can interact in a healthy and personal way without creating all kinds of complex, often indefinable energy flows. The more transparent and more visible each person, organization, and system manifests itself, the easier and simpler they are to deal with. Keep the ability to make your own choices and take responsibility for them.

I realize this is a somewhat simplistic view of things, but it is precisely this simplicity that makes it powerful and universal. The vagueness and abstraction of bureaucracies, the complexity and ambiguity of a legal system or a tax system, and being part of an untraceable algorithmic system creates a dependency. From that dependency, it is impossible to make independent and autonomous choices and take responsibility. Not to mention the increasing dominance of digitization and artificial intelligence.

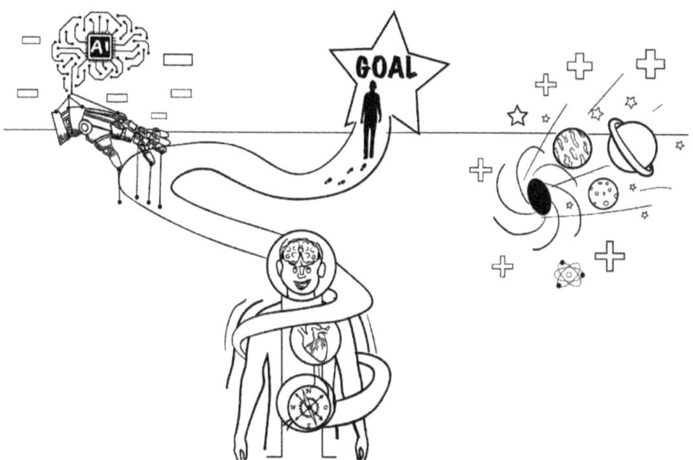

As previously mentioned, I am a big proponent of *keep it smart and simple*, especially of measurable, tangible, and perceptible matters. At its core, life is not complex. We humans often make it complex through the many stories and beliefs we create and maintain throughout our lives. By becoming aware of these, we can make conscious choices and gain the freedom to determine which steps to take, in which direction, and with what magnitude. Or the freedom to choose to take a moment to pause, feel, and think if everything still aligns: to see if everything is still on board and if the course is still correct or may be influenced by a changed circumstance or expectation.

At its core, it is always about moving with awareness. And above all, not making it too big and complex. A small change can already have a significant impact on the future.

Everyone knows the story of the butterfly that flaps

its wings in a tropical area, subtly moving the air, which can eventually grow into a hurricane. The same applies to the game of golf: if you hit the ball with a deviation of only 1-2 millimeters, the result at 200 meters can be a deviation of 20-40 meters.

Perhaps the most practical and powerful example you can immediately realize, experience, and feel right now is when you lift the corners of your mouth by 2 mm. It immediately changes your energy and the way you interact with your surroundings. The most remarkable result is that you immediately experience happiness and are no longer able to think negatively!

Do you see what the impact of keeping it smart and simple on your energy balance is and how it directly affects your quality of life?

You have more knowledge and wisdom at your disposal to take control of your life than you might think. Start using this from now on, no matter how challenging or exciting it is at first. Give energy to the things that are important to you and that you know deep down: yes, this is right!

Follow that intuition from your heart and with your mind. Look at 'what is' instead of 'what is not'. This is a challenge, considering how dominant the control structures and systems are that we have inadvertently and often unconsciously entered into with all good intentions. These make you dependent and only provide false certainties.

Move, take small or big steps, or take a moment to pause. There are no good or bad, better or worse steps. Moving with a goal is already sufficient. Stop with the doubts, the stories, the beliefs, the destructive judgments about yourself, and the fearful thoughts about what is usually not reality.

Connect with people who want and do the same from authenticity. Or 'entice' people to join you, from each person's uniqueness, personal strength, and energy, but never do it from a place of lack or dependency. You will soon notice that the whole is greater than the sum of its parts. When that happens, it is magic, and you get the feeling of coming home in a situation or energy, something we all know in our lives. The birth of a child, that concert where everything around you seemed to disappear, that evening on the dance floor that seemed to last forever, the infatuation and that special kiss and lovemaking.

And really, it doesn't all have to be right and perfect at once. We are allowed to learn, and by doing so, we will regain confidence, and eventually, a new healthy automatism arises.

The only important thing is that your energy can flow again with confidence so that you can take and maintain the quality of your life in your own hands.

Living Freely

With Choice Comes Freedom

By taking control into your own hands, you can also direct your energy within the established frameworks and goals. When you do this, you will see that these same frameworks magically dissolve and disappear. Perhaps you have experienced such moments in your life during a concert, a game, a birth, or an intense, intimate moment.

Dependence on people and created systems may initially seem safe and secure, but dependence inherently implies a lack of freedom. Living freely means daring to stand up for yourself and taking responsibility. It means not to shout or dominate but to take up space from your inner strength, keeping it to yourself. This way, you are authentic and can interact healthily with everyone.

Living freely is always temporary. Let the past be; it has happened, and you cannot change it. Take the experiences and lessons learned with you in your backpack. Knowledge is relative, and as you get older, you will realize that the more you think you know, the less you actually know.

You can only walk through the school of life experience by continuing to step, smell, feel, taste, etc. No matter how many books you read or how many trainings you follow, you will have to experience and do it yourself. Only in practice and with the corresponding experiences can you truly develop 'knowing.'

I can tell you and describe how a delicious, ripe, sweet, juicy fruit can taste, but as long as you haven't tasted it yourself, it remains an image and thought. (Psst … do you now see that delicious sweet overripe strawberry/mango before you… What is now your image and feeling ;))

By making contact and connecting with the laws of nature and its elements, a sense of freedom arises. Every person has the tools at their disposal: their senses. By feeling, smelling, tasting, hearing, and seeing in balance (and not just the environment and experiences but also yourself), the stories will disappear, and energy will flow freely in the direction you desire.

What has personally helped and supported me for over a decade is simply ending my daily warm shower with ... cold water! While observing my thoughts and still occasionally feeling the resistance, I do it anyway, no matter how nice the warm shower is. By breathing deeply and thoroughly, I turn the knob and feel until the energy flows well and the cold water feels warm. And when the energy flows, I am on :).

You really have to do things yourself and truly learn and experience them step by step, always choosing the course to take.

It is crucial to keep in mind what is important to you in your life. Is it really about material things and quantity? Or is it about the quality of life? Deep in your heart, you know and feel the answer.

What are the things that have stayed with you? Is it your tax return, the number of cars you have had, the schools you attended with accompanying diplomas, your wardrobe and shoes, the size of your house and garden, the number of days off and vacation?

Or do you remember, probably with a smile on your face, your first love and kiss, that memorable sunset, the birth of your child, your first earned money, the deer that crossed your path, that intense, unexpected hug? That is the true wealth of energy that is still within you, not to be encompassed and possessed but a factual and actual reality.

I also don't know a lot of things, but I know and can clearly state what reality is and what facts are. And some facts, as they often are and feel, I can regularly find inexplicable.

What I consciously strive for as much as possible is to live my life without making a story or belief out of it and sticking to the facts. This makes life qualitatively higher, more manageable, more enjoyable, more connected, and really more fun to step through.

In this way, you can shape your life with healthy energy and freedom and truly live.

You can do that too. Go for it!

The Circle of Life / Epilogue

Always One and Connected

Hopefully, the search is over, and your journey of discovery can begin.

It's not about agreeing or disagreeing, right or wrong. It's about what you want and whether you can do something with this book.

What steps will you take for yourself, simply because you can and want to… and therefore also 'must'? ;)

The essence is to be aware of what is and, with the tools you now have, to make your choices. By accepting what is—the only thing that is—and realizing that you have the power to live your life as it fits you, the energy will flow in the direction you desire. You can then let go of old patterns and conditionings and begin to manifest what you truly want.

As long as it feels right for you and you are taking the right steps. And remember: if it doesn't feel right yet, it's not the end.

Stop acting out of fear and start acting out of love, with your heart open, according to the natural laws of the Earth and the universe. Realize that you are not just the form of a human being but made up of molecules and atoms, held together in an immense energy of 'emptiness.' A vast emptiness, just like in the universe, which connects us all, including each .other. Call it love or one pot of God, but realize that it is through this that we are always one and connected, All-One!

Things to Pause and Reflect on Daily

- The proof of the pudding is in the eating.
- You can lead the horse to the water but can't let her drink
- Behind the clouds, the sun still shines.
- When the wind is against you, start tacking.
- When the wind is stronger, make sure you are smarter.
- Without dreams, there are no plans, no goals, no energy flow.
- Everything you give attention to grows, and everything that grows will bloom.Your home is your castle, zorg daar onvoorwaardelijk goed voor!
- A kick in the butt and a big hug.
- Never compare yourself to your neighbors, even if their grass seems greener.
- Bears on the road? Give them a big, warm hug.
- I'll take care of you, will you take care of me?
- Observing can happen in four directions, across many layers and currents, on the path to the core. There, everything is whole—love, God.

- If it's not good yet, it's not the end.
- The search has ended, the journey of discovery continues.
- Need to have or want to have?
- Everything comes and goes, and everything is temporary.
- There is never anything other than this moment and where you are right now.

About the Autor

Jules Pieters is a father of four, a partner, a dedicated family man, and a nature enthusiast. His adventurous spirit and deep connection with nature serve as sources of inspiration and insight. As an author, he offers practical tools based on personal experiences and insights aimed at achieving a balance between rational thinking and authenticity.

Jules's writing reflects his journey and the lessons he's learned, providing readers with the means to take control of their lives, break free from old patterns, and create new, healthier habits. His approach is grounded in a blend of traditional and alternative paths, offering a unique perspective on personal growth and self-reliance

The Following Parts in this Series are in Preparation:

Psst … You Have a Choice!

- Workbook "Psst … You Have a Choice!"
- Relations
- Raising Children
- Work That Doesn't Suit You
- The Power of Breathing
- On Weight
- On Communication
- Healthy Living
- Social Media
- Meditation
- Pain and Masochism
- Living Together
- 2 mm is Enough
- Therapy
- School/Learning
- Stories and Dreams
- Mindfucking/Don't Think, Just Act

www.ingramcontent.com/pod-product-compliance
Lightning Source LLC
LaVergne TN
LVHW051054180726
843512LV00019B/1473